Animals 2 Grayscale Adult Coloring Book

Compiled by Renee Davenport

Copyright

The contents of this book are copyrighted
in their present and altered format.
The images were compiled and developed to
create a grayscale coloring book.

© 2018

ISBN-
10: 1-949152-01-4

ISBN-
13: 978-1-949152-01-2

Tinker Bell

Bailey & Friends

There are 8 bonus pages
of sweet pets from the spectacular
Joyful Coloring Books Team.
The team and their pets are ~
Karen Hirshal ~ Vega
Loraine Wilson ~ Oscar
Angie Hardy ~ Tinker Bell
Rosemary Henry ~ Luna
Lynda Rodriguez ~ Oreo
Teddi Krock ~ Mycroft
Carol Wacek ~ Libby
Millie Plastaras ~ Bailey

Thank you for coloring Animals 2 Grayscale Adult Coloring Book

Compiled by Renee Davenport

CPSIA information can be obtained
at www.ICGtesting.com
Printed in the USA
LVHW022113200820
663618LV00010B/746